12|00

BIG CATS

LIONS

Don Middleton

The Rosen Publishing Group's
PowerKids Press™
New York

This book is dedicated to my wife Sue and my daughters Jody and Kim. Without their support, my writing and other wildlife adventures would not have been possible. Also, a special thanks to author and friend Diana Star Helmer for believing in me.

Published in 1999 by The Rosen Publishing Group, Inc.
29 East 21st Street, New York, NY 10010

First Edition

Book Design: Danielle Primiceri

Photo Credits: Cover © 1997 Digital Vision Ltd.;p. 4 © Ronn Maratea/International Stock; pp. 6–7 © Bob Jacobson/International Stock; p. 8 © Maratea/International Stock; pp. 11, 12, 15, 19 © Mark Newman/International Stock; p. 16 © Michele & Tom Grimm/International Stock; p. 20 © Greg Edwards/International Stock; p. 22 © Andre Hote/International Stock.

Middleton, Don.
    Lions / by Don Middleton.
        p.   cm. — (Big cats)
    Includes index.
    Summary: Provides a simple introduction to the physical features, life cycle, and habits of lions.
    ISBN 0-8239-5208-8
    1. Lions—Juvenile literature. [1. Lions.] I. Title. II. Series: Middleton, Don. Big cats.
  QL737.C23M5438 1998
  599.757—dc21
                                                97-32690
                                                   CIP
                                                     AC

Manufactured in the United States of America

CONTENTS

WILD CATS

Lions are the second largest of the wild cats. Only tigers are bigger. There are 37 **species** (SPEE-sheez) of wild cats. Lions are one of the four "great cats."

4

The other great cats are tigers, **leopards** (LEH-perdz), and **jaguars** (JA-gwarz). Only the great cats can give a mighty roar.

Today lions live only in Africa and India. But long ago lions lived all around the world. **Scientists** (SY-en-tists) who study dinosaur bones have found very old lion bones in the United States.

◀ A male lion's mane can range in color from light yellow to brownish-black.

KING OF THE BEASTS

The mane of an African lion, such as this one, is thicker than the mane of an Asian lion.

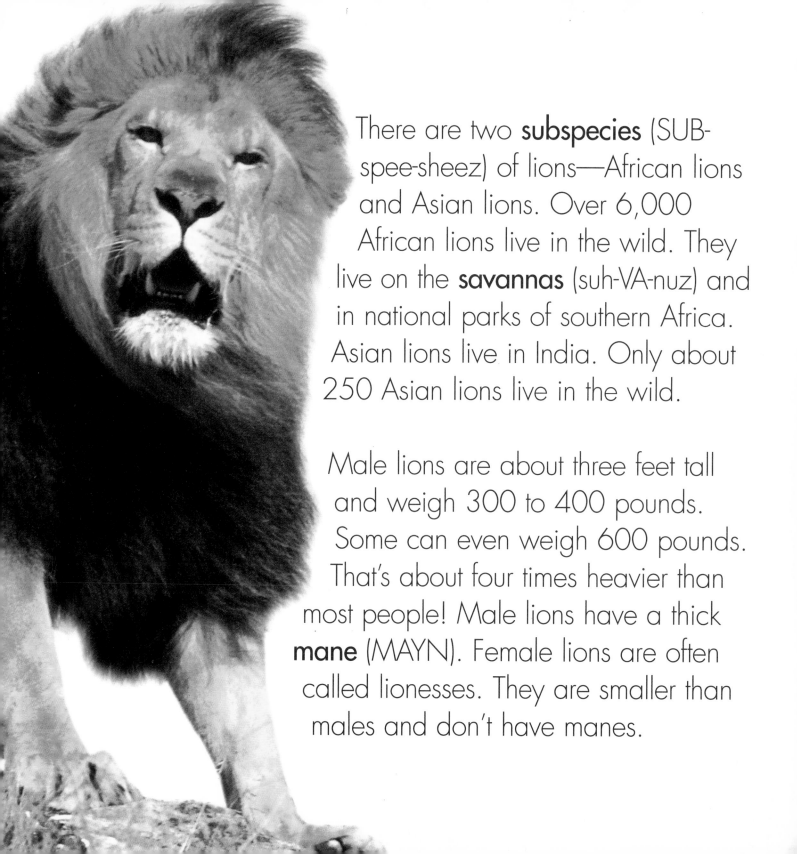

There are two **subspecies** (SUB-spee-sheez) of lions—African lions and Asian lions. Over 6,000 African lions live in the wild. They live on the **savannas** (suh-VA-nuz) and in national parks of southern Africa. Asian lions live in India. Only about 250 Asian lions live in the wild.

Male lions are about three feet tall and weigh 300 to 400 pounds. Some can even weigh 600 pounds. That's about four times heavier than most people! Male lions have a thick **mane** (MAYN). Female lions are often called lionesses. They are smaller than males and don't have manes.

ONE BIG FAMILY

Lions are the only wild cats that do not like to live alone. Lions like to live together in a family group called a **pride** (PRYD). A pride is made up mostly of female lions and their cubs. A pride may have up to 35 lions. All the lionesses in the pride are mothers, sisters, aunts, or cousins to one another.

The pride has only a few adult male lions. They are often brothers from another pride. Their main job is to keep the female lions and cubs in the pride safe from enemies.

These female pride members will watch out for each other and help one another for their entire lives. ▶

FANGS AND CLAWS

Lions are **carnivores** (CAR-nih-vorz). They must eat lots of meat to stay strong and healthy. Lions sleep or rest most of the day. They hunt mostly at night. But if the pride needs food, they will hunt during the day too.

Moving slowly and quietly, lions sneak through the tall grass. Once they are close to their **prey** (PRAY), the lions run toward it very quickly. They use their sharp claws to grab the animal. Then they kill it by biting it on the neck. When they hunt, lions can run up to 35 miles per hour. That's as fast as a car! They can also jump twelve feet in a single leap.

◄ Lions have strong jaws that make it possible for them to kill and eat large prey.

TEAMWORK

Every lion in a pride has a job. The females are usually the hunters. While they hunt, an adult lion guards the cubs. Working as a team, the females hunt zebras and other large animals. The male lions get to eat first. The cubs eat last.

The male lion's job is to protect the land where the pride lives. Males watch for leopards and **hyenas** (hy-EE-nuz) that will eat lion cubs or steal food that the lionesses have caught. They will also fight to keep other male lions away from the pride.

This lioness is getting ready to chase her prey across the savanna. After she makes the kill, the lioness will drag the prey back to the pride, where all the lions will eat.

▼

BABY LIONS

Female lions will **mate** (MAYT) with one of the male lions. Four months later the lioness gives birth. She will have between two and five cubs. Blind and helpless, the cubs are very small. The mother lion hides them from other animals. The cubs have brown fur covered with spots. This helps them hide in the tall grass.

The cubs spend their time sleeping or drinking their mother's milk. While the mother is away hunting, the cubs learn to stay very still and quiet. They meow happily when their mother returns.

These cubs will grow up playing with their brothers, sisters, and cousins in the pride. ▶

GROWING UP

When they are two months old, the lion cubs come out of hiding. Their mother takes them to meet the rest of the pride. At first the cubs are scared. But soon they relax and start to play with the other cubs.

The cubs learn to hunt by watching the adult lionesses closely. The cubs practice hunting grasshoppers, butterflies, and small animals. When the cubs are one year old, they follow the adult females on hunting trips. When they grow up, the female cubs will stay with the pride. But once the male cubs reach about three and a half years old, they leave the pride. The males then go to find their own pride to protect.

◄ Older cubs play games with each other to help them learn to hunt well.

LIONS AND PEOPLE

Today few people are attacked by lions. However, many years ago in an African country called Tanzania, a pride of lions hunted people for food. In fifteen years the lions killed over 1,000 people in Tanzania. Finally the lions had to be killed to protect the people.

In lion country, it is wise to stay in your car or truck. This keeps you safe. But lions are not always safe from humans. **Poachers** (POH-cherz) kill lions **illegally** (il-LEE-gul-lee). They sell parts of the lion, such as teeth, claws, and fur, for money.

In some wildlife parks in Africa, people can watch lions from the safety of a truck. This allows people and scientists to ▶ study the lions and take pictures of them.

Lions that live in a zoo can survive until they are about twenty years old.

LIONS IN ZOOS

Unless you live in Africa or India, the only place to see a real lion is at the zoo. Many zoos try to make the lion's living areas just like their natural **habitats** (HAB-ih-tats). These areas have tall grass, shady spots, and places where the lions can hide and play.

The number of Asian lions in the wild is getting very small. Zoos are helping by sharing and trading lions. This allows Asian lions to mate and have strong, healthy cubs. Perhaps one day the cubs can be released into the wild in India.

A FUTURE FOR LIONS

Lions are an **endangered** (en-DAYN-jerd) species. More lions die each year than are being born. Asian lions are in the most trouble. The Gir Forest in India is the only place left where they still live. In Africa the lions are protected in wildlife parks. But there aren't enough parks to protect all the lions.

We must make sure that lions have large wild places where they and their families can live free and safe.

22

GLOSSARY

carnivore (CAR-nih-vor) An animal that eats other animals for food.

endangered (en-DAYN-jerd) In danger of no longer existing.

habitat (HAB-ih-tat) The place where an animal lives.

hyena (hy-EE-nuh) A dog-like carnivore who lives in the same area as lions.

illegal (il-LEE-gul) Against the law.

jaguar (JA-gwar) One of the four species of great cats. They live in Central and South America.

leopard (LEH-perd) One of the species of great cats. They live in Africa and Asia.

mane (MAYN) Long, thick fur around the neck of a male lion.

mate (MAYT) A special joining of a male and female body. After mating, the female may have a baby grow inside her body.

poacher (POH-cher) A person who kills animals that are protected by law.

prey (PRAY) An animal that is eaten by another animal for food.

pride (PRYD) A group of lions who live together.

savanna (suh-VA-nuh) An area of grassland with few trees and bushes.

scientist (SY-en-tist) A person who studies the way things are and act in the world and the universe.

species (SPEE-sheez) A group of animals that are very much the same.

subspecies (SUB-spee-sheez) A group of animals that are very similar but have some differences.

WEB SITES:

You can learn more about lions on the Internet! Check out these Web sites:

http://wkweb4.cableinet.co.uk/alic/gallery.htm/

http://www.primenet.com/~brendel/

INDEX